D1685624

WHAT'S THE OPPOSITE?

A TURN-AND-SEE BOOK

by Cari Meister

raintree
a Capstone company — publishers for children

6000500178

Opposites are everywhere!
A fire is hot. Ice cubes are cold.
Hot and cold are opposites.
Candy floss is sweet.
Lemons are sour. Sweet
and sour are opposites.

Let's discover more opposites!
Read the text, look at the
picture, and guess the
opposite. Then turn the page
and see if you are right!

Raj and Amy are lifting weights in PE. It is a lot of work! The weights are **heavy!**

What is the opposite of heavy?

Light! Carolina lifts
Mr Cuddles into the air.
He is light and fluffy.

It is a beautiful afternoon for a **slow** walk home from school. Jiah and Aiden take their time and enjoy the weather.

What is the opposite of slow?

turn and see

Fast! Max runs fast to launch the kite in the air. Whoosh!

Rishan chooses three chapter books from the library. Right now the books are **closed**.

What is the opposite of closed?

turn and see

Open! These kids couldn't wait to open their books!

The Harris kids are playing in the park. They jump **over** the rope.

What is the opposite of over?

Under! Kaleb leads the relay team. He crawls under the foam noodles. Go, Kaleb, go!

Dara loves horses! She gets a giant stuffed horse for her birthday. She is **happy**.

What is the opposite of happy?

turn and see

Sad. Maisy cannot go with her older sister to Brownie camp. She is sad.

Yum! The Allen family is roasting marshmallows over a **hot** campfire.

What is the
opposite of hot?

turn and see

Cold! The Yazzie cousins dress up warm for a cold day of sledging. Ready, set, go!

Kezzie patiently waits her turn. The light is red, and red means stop.

What is the opposite of stop?

turn and see

Go! Kezzie hits the pedal as soon as the light turns green. Zoom!

It's match day! **Before** the match, the team meets in a huddle.

What is the
opposite of before?

turn and see

After! After the game, the team celebrates!

Sun and sand are all you need for a fun beach day! Dreyana and her mum are making a **small** sandcastle.

What is the opposite of small?

turn and see

Big! Wow! Look at Trevon and Hailey's sandcastle!

Samir is thirsty after playing outside. He fills his cup to the top. The cup is **full**.

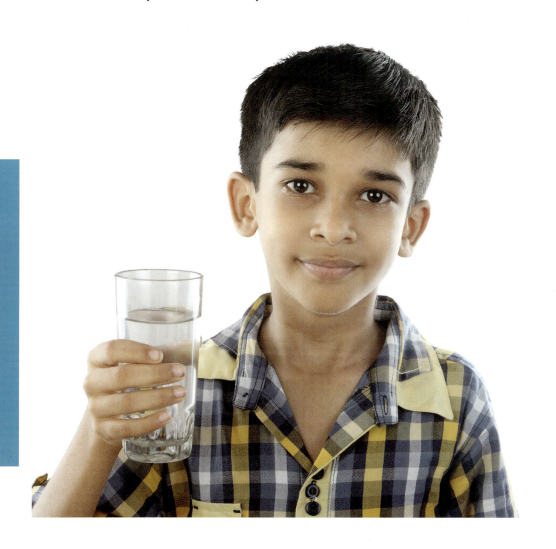

What is the
opposite of full?

turn and see

Empty. Sean gulped down all of his milk. Now the glass is empty.

Woof! Woof! Toby is having a bath. He is very **wet**!

What is the opposite of wet?

turn and see

Dry! Tita's dog, Mr Pickles, ran outside in the rain. Tita used a warm towel to dry him off.

It's street art **day**! The neighbourhood kids from Sunny Drive create a chalk picture.

What is the opposite of day?

turn and see

Night! John and Sidney get ready to camp for the night. Sleep tight!

On a hot summer's day, Emi splashes in her **shallow** pool.

What is the
opposite of shallow?

turn and see

Deep! Noah and his friends dive into the deep end of the pool.

Wah! Wah! Baby Avery is hungry.
She is **loud!**

What is the
opposite of loud?

turn and see

Quiet. Shhh. Baby Quentin is sleeping.

OPPOSITES REVIEW

- heavy/light
- slow/fast
- closed/open
- over/under
- happy/sad
- hot/cold
- stop/go

- before/after
- small/big
- full/empty
- wet/dry
- day/night
- deep/shallow
- loud/quiet

Raintree is an imprint of Capstone Global Library Limited, a company incorporated in England and Wales having its registered office at 264 Banbury Road, Oxford, OX2 7DY – Registered company number: 6695582

www.raintree.co.uk
myorders@raintree.co.uk

Image Credits
Getty Images: FatCamera, 3; Imgorthand, 28, kali9, 7; Obradovic, 24; PeopleImages, 19; THEPALMER, 23; Shutterstock: Alexander_Safonov, 4; ALIAKSANDRKAZLOUSKY, 12; Asia Images Group, 11; BNMK 0819, 22; Brocreative, 5; Jaren Jai Wicklund, 14; leungchopan, 29; mantinov, 27; oliveromg, 13; Peyker, 15, 16; Pixel-Shot, 30; Pond Saksit, 9; Rawpixel.com, 17, 18; RonTech3000, 26; Sergey Novikov, 6, 10, 20, 25; Shyamalamuralinath, 21; tdee photo cm, cover; wavebreakmedia, 8

Editorial Credits
Editor: Christianne Jones; Designer: Tracy McCabe; Media Researcher: Morgan Walters; Production Specialist: Kathy McColley
Printed and bound in India

ISBN: 978 1 3982 1551 1 (hardback)
ISBN: 978 1 3982 1575 7 (paperback)

British Library Cataloguing in Publication Data:
A full catalogue record for this book is available from the British Library.